Dear Baby Preemie

A Miracle in the NICU

by

JACQUE LAMONT HERMAN

WestBow Press books may be ordered through booksellers or by contacting:

WestBow Press
A Division of Thomas Nelson & Zondervan
1663 Liberty Drive
Bloomington, IN 47403
www.westbowpress.com
844-714-3454

All Scripture quotations are taken from the King James Version.

ISBN: 978-1-6642-6140-2 (sc)
ISBN: 978-1-6642-6141-9 (e)

Print information available on the last page.

WestBow Press rev. date: 4/27/2022

WESTBOW
PRESS®
A DIVISION OF THOMAS NELSON
& ZONDERVAN

Introduction Page

For thou art my hope, O Lord God; thou art my trust from my youth.

By thee have I been up holden up from the womb; Thou art he that took me out of my mother's bowels; my praise shall be continually of thee.

I am as a wonder unto many; but thou art my strong refuge.

Let my mouth be filled with thy praise and with thy honor all the day.

Cast me not off in the time of old age; forsake me not when my strength faileth.

Psalms 71:5-9 King James Version

And thou, son of man, be not afraid of them, neither be afraid of their words, though briers and thorns be with thee, and thou dost dwell among scorpions; be not afraid of their words, nor be dismayed at their looks, though they be a rebellious house.

And thou shalt speak my words unto them, whether they will hear, or whether they will forbear; for they are most rebellious.

But thou, son of man, hear what I say unto thee;

Be not thou rebellious like that rebellious house; open thy mouth, and eat that I give thee.

Ezekial 2:6-8 King James Version

Dear Baby Preemie,

I was just like you.

Small and weighing nothing

But God saw me through.

I was born 2lbs and 2 ounces.

I resembled a rat.

I could be cradled in my father's palm and that was that.

My skin began pealing,

a tentative blood transfusion,

and a heart monitor was assigned.

As I reflect, those trials are what God aligned.

I lived in an incubator with bubble wrap as a blanket.

That is entirely true.

My parents and family wondered, "Will this little fellow make it through?"

Wisdom and prayers and intelligence filled my room.

The doctors were guided divinely.

The Creator knew what to do.

"Don't worry parents this child belongs to me.

I've got a plan for him.

You just wait and see."

Hours before my birth, my mom walked a San Francisco hill to the hospital's door.

She simply needed to check her vitals.

My parents had not idea what was in store.

My mother had a small discomfort.

That was truly it.

The doctor said, "The baby is coming! Call your husband quick!"

Dad worked for a bank but when he heard the sound.

No nickel, dime or Jefferson could distract him from being around.

From the beginning of his journey my father dreamed of this moment.

He would not be delayed.

He was going to be a father.

What a joyous day.

At the hospital and surrounded by a team

the physicians prescribed medication that made my mother scream.

The doctor said, "Here take this shot and add that pill too."

Later in my life dad said, "Your mother looked like a blimp
and she ingested those medicines for you."

My mother, as she labored, was writhing in pain.

She screamed, scratched, and even kicked a nurse out the room in distain.

To my mother's defense the nurse was chewing gum and the smell was revolting.

Nevertheless, my birth was catapulting.

My mother yearned for her mother which made my dad feel a certain way.

But all egos aside

The 17th of January was my special day.

"He's here!" said the nurse. "The little *French* prince!"

I'm not French but I was named after the great explorer Jacques Cousteau

My life would be deemed for exploration and keeping people in the know.

Time will do its thing, and parents please preserver.

You may visit the NICU daily and always be of good cheer.

Dad, you will have to carry Mom because your child is hers.

Mom, you will need to pray for Dad as he sets the vision for your futures.

You, as parents, are only human and I know your child is on your minds.

Think joyfully of diapers, toys and living life sublime.

As you journey through this ordeal remember to have grace.

Keep a restaurant in mind when you need to fix your face.

Your child belongs in God's hands. He knows the plans for them.

Allow His will to be done and the purposes from Him.

Dear Baby Preemie, I was just like you.

Many years later,

Just look at what God can do!

Never the End

A Note from the Author to NICU Parents:

My parents, Gerald and Cynthia Herman deserve their flowers and so do you. Having a special need child with complications so early is not ideal but it does happen. That's why I needed to write this book. You are not alone in your physical and emotional experiences. My parents struggled and were forced to endure. You will need the strength of God to do the same.

I was born in 1985 at the beginning of the AIDS epidemic. As a result of this my parents received a letter that the blood transfusion I was given could have been tainted with the HIV virus. This report turned out negative, thank God, but the toll that each new development took on my parents was chaotic. My skin was too sensitive to touch and I wasn't released from the NICU until four months later after I had gained 5lbs. My parents had to also bare the pain of other NICU parents as their children did not survive. When I finally did get home my heart would drop as I slept alarming the whole house with a siren. Times were exhausting for my family.

Nevertheless, I now work for the same company that diagnosed me at birth with a 50% chance to live. Kaiser Permanente has always been a staple in my life. I am grateful for their support.

Put your trust in God for your baby. Whatever the outcome please know that even if it hurts, God's plans are not to harm you but to give you hope and a future. I love you and I'm praying for your journey. Be blessed.

Jacque Lamont Herman

Acknowledgements

My first fruits of gratitude go to the servant of servants the Lord Jesus Christ. I am ecstatic to be saved, sanctified and filled with the Holy Ghost. I enjoy being called His and to serve Jesus in my own special way. He called me to encourage His flock and I am so grateful to operate in my gift.

A great thank you to my wife Tara.

My Parents Gerald, Cynthia, and Veronica.

My brother Jerron Herman

My grandparents: Mary, Richard, Stanley, Ann, Sylvia, Eunice.

My Aunts: Gwen, Bonnie, Madonna, Lumumba, Hilda, Stacy, Emme, Shonda, Daphne, Lisa, Bettie, Caroline, Jean

My Uncles: Kim, Keith, Tony Dabney, Neal Cherry, Richard, Sam, Herbert, King David.

A thunderous shout out to all my illustrious Cousins.

Thank you to my fantastic friend/ sister/ agent Ms. Yolonda Franklin.

Editors Jessie Dillon, Akelah Trinay and Jerhetta Suite

My early illustrators Andre Chris Neal and Issa Day Simmons

To the ladies that diligently prayed me through the NICU: Denise Davis, "Tia" Toni Powell, Roxanne Roberts, Brenda Salsberry, Regina Wilson, Renata Phillips and Leslie Poole.

A special thank you to each house of prayer:

Pastor Williams and Pastor Hawkins and all the members of Neighborhood Baptist Church of San Francisco, Ca.

Bishop Bob Jackson and the members of Acts Full Gospel Church of God in Christ of Oakland, Ca.

Pastor and First Lady Manning of Pasadena Church of God

Pastor and First Lady Hearn and all the valued family of Lincoln Avenue Celestial Temple Church of God in Christ, Pasadena, CA

Bishop Roy Dixon and the Fourth Evangelistic Jurisdiction.

To my fraternal squad: Parkers, Ivorys, Hayes, Porters, Isreals, Vincent, Hodges, Browns, Hearns, Knights, Hennings, Tuffin.

A special thank you to my friends: Alonso Reyes, David Morgan Jr, Deb Lazor, and Jeannette Franco Kushner who when I mentioned I was writing this book asked "Where do I get my copy?" Thank you for the early vote of confidence.

Thank you to all the establishments and quality professionals that nurtured my mind, body, and personality:

Loving and Caring Day Care, Fellowship Academy of San Francisco, Paden Elementary of Alameda Ca, Encinal High School of Alameda Ca, California State University, Los Angeles and CSULA Theater Arts Department, Pasadena Playhouse, Kaiser Permanente Health Care Organization and Kaiser Permanente's Southern California Educational Theater.

Lastly Thank you West Bow Press for this very special opportunity to help publish the work of God in my life.

Dear Baby Preemie is dedicated to my nephews Joshua, Preston and Prayer and my nieces Victoria, Harper, and Knolle. NICU stories are real and everyone with a story deserves to be heard and shown empathy.

Blessed is the man that walketh not in the counsel of the ungodly, nor standeth in the way of sinners, nor sitteth in the seat of the scornful.

But his delight is in the law of the Lord; and in his law doth he meditate day and night.

And he shall be like a tree planted by the rivers of water, that bringeth forth his fruit in his season; his leaf also shall not wither; and whatsoever he doeth shall prosper.

Psalms 1:1-3 King James Version

Printed in the United States
by Baker & Taylor Publisher Services